Women

I Have Known & Been

Women

I HAVE KNOWN & BEEN

CAROL LYNN PEARSON

 ASPEN BOOKS

Women I Have Known and Been

No portion of this book may be reproduced in any form without written permission from the publisher, Aspen Books, 6211 South 380 West, Salt Lake City, UT 84107.

Library of Congress Cataloging-in-Publication Data

Pearson, Carol Lynn.
    Women I have known & been / Carol Lynn Pearson.
        p. cm.
    ISBN 1-56236-306-9 (alk. paper)
    1. Women—Poetry. I. Title. II. Title: Women I have known and been.
    PS3566.E227W6 1992
    811'.54—dc20   92-9920
                                                                    CIP

Printed in the United States of America

10 9 8 7 6 5 4 3 2 1

Cover design: Brian Bean
Painting: Shauna Cook Clinger

CONTENTS

WOMEN AND THEMSELVES

Creation Continued 2
Picture Window 4
Baking Bread 6
Beautiful 8
Dreams 10
Ms. Mead Said So 11
This is Not What Susan B. Anthony Had in Mind . . 12
Mary Ann 13
Single 14
Throw It Away 16
Support Group 24
Power 25
Cousin Helen 26
Battered Woman 28
Hungry Child 30
Breakthrough 31
Obedient Girl 32
Relegated to the Kitchen 33
History's Affirmative Action 34
High 35
The Sins of the Fathers 36
Her Father's Tears 50
New Hands 52
Woman Aging 53
Still Life 54
A Dream of Peace 56

WOMEN AND THEIR MEN

I Speak For Romantic Love 60
What You Do To Me 62
Sabbath 64
Essence of Love 65
Focus 66
Filling You 67
Bearable 68
Like Mistletoe 69

For a Daughter in Love ....
Mother and Other Child ....
Falling Out of Love Haiku ....
" . . . and Obey" ....
Shopper ....
After the Mastectomy ....
Flaws ....
Split ....
Radical ....
Carla and Jim ....
Position ....
Supportive Wife ....
Wrong, Right? ....
Suttee For Richard's Wife ....
Turning ....
To the Truth: Invitation That Was Never Sent .....
The Rain and the Ground ....
Letting Go ....
Not a Pair ....
Unborn ....
She Waited ....
Second Wedding ....
Last Touch ....

WOMEN AND THEIR CHILDREN

Bankers ....
Matriarchal Blessing ....
Motherload ....
Child Making ....
Aaron's Other Woman ....
In Celebration of the First Menstruation ....
Christ Children ....
Child-Raising Seminar ....
Don's Daughter ....
Forever Child ....
Clean ....
On Purpose ....
Mother's Post Pledge ....
Don't Push ....
For Children Grown and Gone ....
John Leaves Home ....
Raja Motherhood ....

Women

AND

Themselves

CREATION CONTINUED

I will continue
To create the universe today
Right where God left off.

Little pockets of chaos
Somehow survived the ordering
And I feel moved
To move upon them
As in the beginning
The Spirit of God moved
Upon the face of the waters.

I will move upon my backyard today
And the weeds will be subdued
And the flowers can grow
And it will be good.

I will move long-distance
Upon a broken heart
And leave a little balm
And it will be good.

I will move upon
The hunger of my children
With salad and spaghetti
Which is Emily's favorite
And it will be good
And even they will say so.
And I will move too
Upon their minds

Leaving a little poem
Or an important thought
And that will be even better
Though they won't say so.

I will move upon
Birth defects and AIDS
With five and ten dollar checks
To help the scientists
Who are battling the big chaos
And I will move upon world hunger
With a twenty-four dollar check
For little Marilza in Brazil
And it will be good.

I will move upon
The kitchen floor
And the dirty laundry
And a blank piece of paper
And at the end of the day
Have a little creation to show.

And the evening and the morning
Are my eighteen thousand
And ninety-sixth day
And tomorrow will start another one.
And here is chaos and there is chaos
And who knows if creation
Will finally be done?

PICTURE WINDOW

Kathleen
Who was out of control
Like a slope of oranges
After someone has taken
Ten at the bottom
Looked enviously at

Susan
Who carried her stress
As gracefully as she carried
The perfect pie
She had brought to the meeting
Last Wednesday night.

Kathleen
Who yelled at her children
Even when they were not
In danger of oncoming cars
And who slammed the door
After she told her husband
To have it his way then
And who once a week at least
Locked herself in the bathroom
And cried
Called

Susan
Who never perspired
And who taught classes called
"Toward a More Feminine You"

And who smiled all the time
And whose children
Always got awards
To ask if she could
Come over sometime
To get a little help.

Kathleen
Who was so disorganized
That she went on Thursday
Instead of Friday
Got a lot of help from

Susan
Who happened to be
Out front in curlers
And wrinkled slacks
And wild-woman eyes
Screaming at her youngest child
Who had just batted a ball
Through the picture window
That framed the lamp
With the beautiful butterflies.

BAKING BREAD

There seemed more accusation
Than admiration
In Vivian's voice
When she said,
"Well, I wish *I* had time
To bake bread!"

And so sometimes when
The loaves were in the oven
And Vivian was at the door
Louise mumbled something about
Another bake sale again

And never even tried to explain
Her near-religious ritual:

How the flour on her fingers
Was the sun and the rain
And the earth

How the thump of her palms
On the dough
Was the dance of women
On the ancient threshing floor

How the smell of the baking
Leavened her
And left her believing that
We rise, we rise

And
How the cutting
Of the first warm slice
For the first child home
Made her a bounteous goddess
With life in her hand.

BEAUTIFUL

Julie wanted to be beautiful
As a man in the desert wants water.

She wanted to be beautiful
And she wanted people to say she was beautiful
And so Julie finally clipped from the paper
The little ad about Alexander's
Modeling Agency that she'd almost
Clipped out every morning for a month
As she studied it over her cereal and toast.

On the fifteenth
Alexander examined Julie's knockout eyes
And good brows and let down her ponytail
So that the long, blond hair fell Rapunzel-like
Nearly to her twenty-two inch waist
And he circled her five feet nine
One hundred and twenty pound body
Like an auctioneer and told her she was
Fantastic and to come back when
She had taken off ten
And wrote her down for a return
On the thirtieth.

On the thirtieth, however,
Julie missed the appointment
As she was suffering the effects
Of a fluke accident brought on by swallowing
A fourth of a box of baking soda
So she could throw up
For the third time that day.

In fact
Two hundred friends and family
Filed by her coffin
Which featured four dozen roses
And many cried and many paused to say
How beautiful she looked.

DREAMS

Martha
Cleaning house
After the last child left
Finds her favorite biology text
And blows dust from the dream
She grew up with.
Is forty-eight too old
To enroll in veterinarian school?

And Georgia
Down the street
Home from board meeting
With a new pile of papers
Wryly smiles
As she pulls from the closet
The oak cradle
She had intended for something
Other than overflow
For her most important files.

MS. MEAD SAID SO

In every tribe
No island excepted

Basket weaving
If done by men
Is hot stuff
Real buff:
Masculine.

And basket weaving
If done by women
Is mere fluff
Not enough:
Feminine.

So women, of course
Are leaving their weaving

And whatever will we
Float the children in?

THIS IS NOT WHAT
SUSAN B. ANTHONY
HAD IN MIND

Down at the high school
Parking lot
The girls smoke
Rings around the boys.

(Twenty percent of females
Who have really
Come a long way
Light up, I read today
And sixteen percent of males.)

And over at the grade school
The children chant
About a pail of water:
"Jack fell down
And broke his crown
And Jill came tumbling after."

MARY ANN

Mary Ann didn't have a man
And she noticed it most
When she bought a new dress.
She noticed there was
No one to notice.

No one to look up
With widened eyes
And smiling say, "Hey, *hey*!"

No one to touch the silk
With an appreciative finger
Or lift the lace a little.

No one to button it up for her
Or unbutton it for himself.

Mary Ann didn't have a man
But didn't notice it as much
In her old clothes.

Whenever she bought a new dress
She looked in the mirror and sighed.

And whenever she bought new pajamas
She cried.

SINGLE

No one could believe Jenny
Was happy living alone
So she soberly accepted their sympathy
Like she accepted other
White elephants
She put in a big box
In the back closet
And thanked them very much

Then clicked the lock quick
As if hiding a secret

And ate a big salad
In front of the whales and dolphins
On PBS

And spent an hour
At her keyboard
Processing her words

And sat twenty minutes
At the window
Watching the storm dance branches

And stayed on the phone
An hour and a half
Until a hundred hungry Africans
Were fed

And then took a bath
Three chapters long

And slept smiling and sprawled
In her queen-size bed.

THROW IT AWAY

The bottles were lined up
Like little soldiers on the bathroom sink.
Sara had ranked them by strength.
The red ones were the killers
And would be sent first
Backed by the green
And then the white.
Together they were the good army
She needed to get it done right.

Left was the half bottle
That had been in the cabinet for years
Which she had got for the biopsy that time
And now a soldier too weak to fight.

She pried off the lid and watched the pills
Drop into the toilet in a single splash.

> *Empty, powerless, useless.*
> *Throw them away!*

She tossed the bottle into the trash.
And her turn was next.

Powerless! She had always been powerless.
Or had she once been potent
But had sat on the shelf too long?

She remembered—was it her?—a girl
Who could run a mile after two dance classes

And stand up to the fourth grade bully
And heal a hamster's broken leg
With a splint and a song.

She remembered a woman who could
Write an "A" paper at two a.m.
And climb a mountain on the steepest side
With more than her share of food on her back
And leave twenty-five love-notes
All over the apartment for a roommate
Whose mother had died.

If that was her it was another lifetime.
She had traded herself for him
And done it gladly for she loved him so.
She overflowed with him
Like a vase that runs a little waterfall
Onto the table—it has so many flowers.

She let him—made him—fill up every space.
Even when he gave her the article
On the women's triathalon, she had said,
"Oh, I don't have time for that,
And I'd rather spend the weekend with you."

She had traded herself for him
And now he was gone and she was empty
And had collapsed around her emptiness
Like a shopping bag without its bread.

It would not be a sin
For she would not be killing a living thing.

She would be weeding the garden
And the weed was dead and brown.
His love had been her greening
And her salvation.

She had searched herself
For something that was still alive
Even seeds she could soak
And she had found nothing.
Only pain would die.

Her children would be better off, surely.
Her brother who had them for a week now
Might keep them then.
She was a bare cupboard to their needs
A broken cup stained with bitterness.
They ought never to taste her again.

> *"Mama, can you french braid*
> *my hair? Mama, what's the*
> *matter? Braid my hair, can't you?"*

> *"No, I can't, I can't, I CAN'T."*

> *Oh, oh, oh, throw it away!*

One desperate day with the want ads
Had made her future clear as a crystal ball:
She was not marketable.
Child support—if he paid—and a minimum wage
From Safeway or the drugstore
Would form the piggy bank they would live on.
She would do her best

To stay awake for an evening class
In maybe dental assisting
And come home to scream
At a child's smallest request.

She would be a little rubber band
Stretched thin to keep house
Job and children together
And if she had to add a broken washing machine,
Snapping!

> *Oh, throw it away, and do it now!*

She turned on the water to fill the glass
And her eyes warily traveled up to the mirror.

> *Oh, God!*

More than an exclamation, it was a prayer.

> *Please, don't let me look like that!*

Her brown hair was oily and uncombed
And flat on the side she'd been lying on.
Her skin was red and puffy
And her eyes were shrunk and sunk in dark hollows.
The yellow bathrobe she'd had on for days
Was torn and tired and she'd hated it
Even when new, but could never justify
Getting a prettier one.

> *Oh, throw it away!*

Her hand picked up the first red bottle
Then paused as she looked again at her face.
Jolene would be the one to find her.
To find her looking like *that?*

Jolene, president of the women's group
At church, had been calling daily
And needed or not was coming by that night.
A picture of what Jolene would find
Moved like a gust of cold wind through Sara's mind.
The least she could do was to tidy up a bit.

Sara filled the tub with hot water
Remembering as it was almost full
The bottle of bubble bath
Her twelve year-old daughter gave her last birthday.
She had been saving it for when
The little one needed a treat
But now she poured a little, then more
Then all and watched the bubbles foam
Their magic pink and gold as if she had
Never seen them before.

Sara lay soaking in the tub
Enjoying it as one enjoys the very last
Chocolate in the box.
She shampooed and conditioned her hair
Letting her fingers caress the scalp just
Like Tina's over at the beauty school
When she went in for a cut.

She hadn't taken a tub bath in maybe a year
Just quick showers because two minutes

Was all it sometimes took
For one child to maim another.

She got out and dried her skin slowly
And smoothed her body with lotion.
The hot rollers were ready and she put them in
Carefully including every hair.
She couldn't bear to put the yellow bathrobe
Around her soft, lotioned skin.

New wine in old bottles!

Wadding and stuffing it into the wastebasket
Made her laugh the first laugh she'd
Had in three months.
She would never need the yellow bathrobe again.

Throw it away!

Now, which dress? The blue one, of course.
People always told her she looked nice
In that dress. It matched her eyes.
Of course, her eyes would be closed
Or would they be open
And Jolene have to close them?

Slowly Sara took out the rollers
And brushed her hair
Teasing it a little to add some height
And trimming the bangs just a little there.

Eye shadow—lip liner—lipstick—mascara.
This would be her thank you to Jolene for caring.

She'd have to remember to lie down
On the couch so as not to muss her hair.
Perfume—lilac, her favorite.

There!

Sara reached again for the red pills
And poured them all into her hand
Then picked up the glass of water and—

Who was that woman in the mirror?
That woman with just a hint of a lover
On her lips and a hint of
A mountain climber in her eye.
Sara studied the woman
Then spoke in slow amazement:

"You look too good to die!"

Suddenly a dam broke
And Sara was no longer empty.
She was filled with rage
Rage against whatever had made
That woman in the mirror feel like a weed
Rage against him for taking
Her power, rage against herself
For giving it away.

She threw the red pills against the wall
And they bounced into the bathtub.

Throw it away!

They were not the soldiers!
She was the soldier
And she would win this war!

She grabbed the next bottle
And threw the pills against the wall.
Smash! The traitors!
She was not the enemy, but they nearly had her.

She would live!
She would fill herself
Quarter inches at a time
Until she was full and real and
Capable
          and beautiful
                    and marketable!

The last of the pills hit the wall
And dropped into the tub
And she bent and turned on the water.
As she watched their little bodies
Swirl down the drain, the phone rang.

"Hello? Jolene? . . .
Yes, you can take me out to lunch. Surprise.
Right now. I'm already dressed.
Oh, anywhere. No . . ."

It must have sounded strange, she thought,
To hear a woman say with a voice
Shaking and sobbing,

          "I . . . want . . . Mexican!"

SUPPORT GROUP

You can fall here.
We are a quilt set to catch you
A quilt of women's hands
Threaded by pain made useful.

With generations of comfort-making
Behind us, we offer this gift
Warm as grandma's feather bed
Sweet as the Heavenly Mother's
Lullaby song.

You can fall here.
Women's hands are strong.

POWER

When she learned that she
Didn't have to plug into
Someone or something
Like a toaster into a wall

When she learned that she
Was a windmill and had only
To raise her arms
To catch the universal whisper
And turn

        turn

           turn

She moved.

Oh, she moved
And her dance was a marvel.

COUSIN HELEN

I know I am related
To the farthest twig
And the last little leaf
On the family tree
From which billions hang
Rooted in Eden.

But it's lovely to be
Clustered close
With just a few
With you and the other
Cousins and aunts and uncles
That sprouted here
Because back there at the
Crook of the branch
Sarah married George.

It's good to share
Similar names and noses
And history.
It's good to have someone
Who has to care
Because our mothers
Would want us to,
An organic obligation
If you will
And then to find we're friends
No matter our genes.

Of all the billions
Like it or not
I'm here, near, yours
And grateful.

BATTERED WOMAN

She was a battered woman
And her other name was Vivian
And her other clothes were home
Because she left with just
Her car keys and her children
After he beat her up again
And this time swore he'd kill her.

She was mine for overnight
Safe on an anonymous couch
Tomorrow in a shelter.

I washed a hairbrush for her
Got a washcloth and towel
And pajamas she could keep
And fixed some supper
After which the two small boys
Ran from room to room
Looking for toys
And Vivian sat on the floor
And watched wrestling.

I gave her Lindberg's *Gift From the Sea*
But she didn't want to read.
I put on my favorite from
"Five Centuries of the Harp"
But she didn't want to listen.

"I like to watch the wrestling," she said.
"I always watch the wrestling."

With bruises still fresh
From being thrown against the wall
And stomped on the floor
And smashed with a chair
Vivian brightened noticeably
As she watched the man with no neck
And a bald head wearing white shorts
Slam onto his back
Like a ham at the butcher's
The man with a beard and an eye patch
Wearing black.

HUNGRY CHILD

She looks at my steamed vegetable dish
Potatoes, cabbage, carrots, onions, mushrooms
Like a tourist looks at raw fish.

She pokes at it, eats a little
Then goes home, creaks up her stair
Opens her cupboard and pulls up her chair
To a real meal:
Reese's P-Nut Butter Cups
Which she had yesterday
And will have tomorrow
Several six-pacs at a time.

I shake her, but she is too big to budge.

I make her go to a doctor
And she may sometime go back.

I take her to the grocery and introduce her
To the broccoli and the grapefruit
And she laughs her nervous laugh
And says hello.

I call, write, threaten, suggest.

Then I give up
And hold her, just hold her
This child of nameless hungers
This frightened child
Silently screaming and desperately clutching
A sweet chocolate breast.

BREAKTHROUGH

She always ignored
The ring of her telephone
Like a private ignores
The bark of his sergeant.

So on the February day that she
Climbed out the upstairs window
To sit on the roof and be only feet
From the full-flowered Magnolia tree

And the telephone rang

And she did not jump and dive
But only stared
At the mass of purple-pink and white petals
Curled friendly around each other
Dancing gently on the air

And the telephone stopped

She sat there
AWOL and smiling.

OBEDIENT GIRL

Everybody was proud of this little girl.
She loved to please and obey.
She got good grades
And she baked good cakes
And she cleaned her room each day

(And she came home pregnant at seventeen).

She loved to please and obey.

RELEGATED TO THE KITCHEN

In the front room
Grandfather and the men
Straightened ties and shoulders
Exchanged business cards
And solutions for the war
Slapped backs at jokes
And were very hungry.

And in the kitchen
Grandmother
And the aproned women
Warmed the hors d'oeuvres
And one another
Hugged, kissed cheeks
Touched each other's hair
Talked heartbreak and hope
And dreams of the day
And were filled
Before the filling
Of the first tray.

HISTORY'S AFFIRMATIVE ACTION

Of course it's not fair
But it may be karma.

Carma
Being a modern woman
Can butter her bread
On both sides
And have her cake
And eat it too
Or even butter her cake
On both sides
Which she is having
And eating too.

I mean
She can sue
Her employer for promoting
A less-qualified male
And on the way home
When she has a flat
Step out in her spikes and hail
The nearest man and bat
Her eyelashes so that
He gets grease on

And she never has to
Break a nail.

HIGH

The high that Glenda felt
After going one more day
And one more day
Without reaching for the pills
After actually getting through
The holidays unanesthetized

Was perhaps not as intense
As the other high
But it had fringe benefits:

It did not make her lie
It did not make her husband cry
And it left her looking
At the woman in the
Medicine cabinet mirror
With a hopeful eye.

THE SINS OF THE FATHERS

Joanna could barely give
The driver his tip
With her shaking fingers
Could barely resist the urge to slip
Back in the cab and return
To the airport and home.

She turned and stared at the house.
She had never come here by taxi before,
Hundreds of times by bicycle
By roller skates, by jump rope
And then, of course, after she was sixteen
And could drive, all the time by car.

The house looked smaller
Than she remembered
And even the willow tree at the window
Of her old room looked as if
It had shrunk in the rain.

The cracks in the sidewalk were the same.
In that one she had lost a fifty-cent piece
And spent hours with a twig trying to get it out
But it was gone forever.
She was almost tempted now to stop
And work on it again
Or to pull a few weeds in the flower bed
Or to walk to the mail box and see
If the mail had come yet—
Anything to put off going in.

Her mother's words long-distance
Still sounded in her ear.

"Joanna, your father's dying."

She had felt the familiar, curdling hate
Move in her stomach and rise to her mouth.

"No, I won't come. I won't."

"Please, Joanna, you must.
Whatever it was, can't you put it away
Now at the end?"

"No, Mother, I can't."

And the taste on her tongue was rust.

Her mother didn't know.
At least, Joanna had pretended her mother
Was as innocent as the row
Of seven year olds she still taught
The sweet parts of the Bible in Sunday School.
But she would soon have to see
The stains on her own hands
For she was a helpmeet to guilt,
A dutiful supporter of sin.

No one knew, no one but a voice
Safe without a face
On the other end of the telephone
Where she had called

Because she read in the paper about
Groups for women like her.
The words had come out in waves like retching
And she had been left shaking
And wiping her mouth.

"Thursday at seven," the voice had said.
"Please come, you should not be alone.
We can help. Promise me you'll come."

"I—I will."

She didn't.

Her husband didn't know.
Glen only knew she hated to have him touch her
That she almost stopped breathing
Had right from the beginning.
But she did the best she could
For he was good man
Far better than she deserved
And if he *did* know he would
Never want to touch her again
Which would be even worse
So she told him nothing.

She had tried once when she was ten
To tell someone at church.

"Joanna!"

He had looked at her shocked as if
She had spat in the sacrament.

"Your father is a good man
A righteous man. You are mistaken
Or you are lying. No . . . no!
Not another word!"

The memories had faded
As memories do when your life depends on it
Faded like a photograph in the sun.
But now, as Joanna stood staring at the house,
They all came back in a rush of pain
And color and sound and smell
And she pressed her hands hard to her chest
As a little moan rose and fell.

Right there, behind the pink flowers
On the white curtains in that room
When her light was out, he would come in.
When she was little she thought
All fathers had "private time"
With their little girls
Like all fathers went to work and mowed the lawn
And played ball with their boys.
And he was her father and she loved him
And she ran to the door when her mother
Came from the kitchen clapping clouds of flour
From her hands and saying, as though it was
A great wonder,

    "Daddy's home!"

So she loved him and he loved her
And she was his little darling
And his good, obedient girl.

And later on, when his coming to her
Made her shake and vomit and imagine
She was a leaf on the willow tree
Outside her window, she begged him not to.
But he said it was his "patriarchal privilege"
And she didn't know what that meant
So she would close her eyes and cry
And he stroked her and said
If she ever told she would die.

So she pushed the dresser
Up against the door at night
Against the sound of his step, against his touch
And she prayed a lot
But they had told her
In Sunday School that God was a father,
So she didn't really trust him much.

The hate went everywhere
Like water from a hose you let go of.
It covered her father: he was drenched in hate.
It covered her mother: why was she
Powerless as a paper doll?
But mostly it covered Joanna.
She was chilled with it
Left still and weeping and despising herself.
Oh, if only she had been a better girl!
If only she had shared her candy bar
When Amy asked on the way home from school
Daddy would not have hurt her that night.
If only she had memorized The Twenty-Third Psalm
Like she was supposed to
She would not be punished so.

As her body got bigger, Joanna got smaller
And the rest of the space filled up with shame
Shame so pressing and hot
That she sawed her skin
With a nail file to try to let it out.

He stopped coming to her when she was fourteen
And they never spoke of it at all
But it hung between them like masses of dark cobwebs
And she would go out of her way
Not to brush against him
At the table or in the hall.

And she left home the day after graduation
And hadn't gone back in ten years
And addressed letters only to her mother
And tried to put it away, put it all away
On a high shelf in a dark closet
But it kept falling out.
It covered her like a light layer of soot
So she didn't like to be looked at.
It moved inside to lodge in her brain
Like a black hole that sucked in the
Words she tried to read in books.
It twisted around her like a snake
And placed its head between her
And the ocean and her and the flower
And her and the Christmas tree ornament
And her and her baby's sweet fingers
And her and Glen, always between her and Glen.

Joanna picked up her suitcase
And walked slowly down the sidewalk

And up the three stairs to the little porch.
Movement made her remember why she had come.
He would not be allowed to go scot-free.
After her mother's phone call
She had sat on the couch reeling with anguish.
Not for him, why should she feel sorry for him?
She only felt sorry that he was going to be free
And never pay in this life, never have to see
The terrible, unhealed wounds she wore every day
And know that his hand had put them there.
Maybe in the next world he would pay
If there really was a hell, but not in this
And it wasn't fair.

If he died scot-free, she would be burdened forever,
Carrying alone the terrible, crushing weight of his sin.
Perhaps, if she could finally give it back to him
Fling his filth in his own face
Make him take it with him to the grave or to God
She could be released.
Maybe if his eye ever acknowledged the wounds
They could begin to heal.

Slowly Joanna opened the door and stepped in.
Pine cleaner and old magazines—
The house still smelled the same.
She stopped in the hall and put down the suitcase.

The picture. Of course it was still there.
Jesus in a bamboo frame
Two Jesuses, really, one at lower left on the cross
Bleeding beneath his crown of thorns
Eyes lifted longingly to heaven

And at the upper right another Jesus
In a white robe before an open tomb
Standing a few inches off the ground
Face glowing like an Easter sunrise.

Sometimes the picture had been all
That had kept her going.
She would bring her little red stool into the hall
And sit looking at it for hours
Talking to Jesus as he hung bleeding on the cross
And he would talk to her.

> "Jesus, do you hurt bad?"

> "Oh, yes, I hurt real bad."

> "I do too, Jesus. I don't think
> I can stand it, I hurt so bad."

> "Well, when you feel that way,
> Joanna, you just come to me
> And I will help you
> Because I'm bigger than you are."

They talked about her father
And about Judas Iscariot
And Joanna came to feel that she was
Jesus' special friend because she understood.
She understood how it felt
To have someone you trusted hurt you.
She understood how it felt to have your body taken
And you can't move and they do what they want.

She learned the word for that in Sunday School:
Crucified.

> "Oh, poor, sweet Joanna," Jesus
>   would say,
> "As soon as I get down from this cross,
> I will help you."

And they talked and talked
And sometimes Jesus would say,

> "They don't know what they're doing,
> You know. We have to forgive them."

But every time he would talk like that
Joanna would take her little red stool
And go back to her room,
Because she didn't understand about forgiving
And she didn't want to.

Remembering that little girl with her
Soft, helpless, violated body
Brought Joanna back to her anger.
That little girl: sacrificed, crucified.

As Joanna opened the door to the back bedroom,
Her mother turned and jumped.

> "Oh, I didn't hear you. Oh, Joanna!"

She hurried across the room
And enfolded her daughter in an embrace.

"I'm so glad you came, so glad!"

"Hello, Mother. How is he?"

"Pretty bad. I hope he'll know you."

"I hope he will."

Joanna looked at the man lying with a sheet
Over him up to his shoulders
And took a tentative step toward the bed.

His arms were folded across his chest
And a pillow propped his head.

Ten years. His hair was a lot thinner
And not dark any more.
And he looked smaller
As if he too had shrunk in the rain.

She would not feel sorry for him.

"Daddy?"

Her voice was shaking.
The sound started tough, but ended soft.

"Daddy? It's me."

Her father's eyes opened
Clouded blue
And looked at her or past her.

> "There are some things you need
> to hear, Daddy."

She had been practicing as if for a school play
And now stage fright left her mouth dry
And her fingers cold.

> "What you did to me, Daddy,
> Was a terrible, vile and
> Inexcusable thing!
> It has been with me every day
> Of my life like a pain that never leaves.
> A father is supposed to protect a child,
> Didn't you know that?
> He's supposed to keep the enemies away,
> Not be the enemy himself!
> Didn't you know you were killing me?
> Didn't you know I would suffer every day
> For the rest of my life?
> Didn't you know I would hate you
> Like I do now? I hate you!
> Oh, Daddy, how I hate you!"

The old man's eyes were wide and wet
And his lips quivered toward speech.
Joanna's mother sobbed quietly behind her.

> "No, no!"

Her father's lips carved out a small sound
And Joanna leaned in.

"What, Daddy?"

"I . . . forgive you."

"What?"

"I forgive you."

Startled, Joanna looked at her mother.

"He's not talking to you, Joanna.
He's talking to them."

"Them?"

"His uncle Robert and his uncle LeRoy.
He's been talking to them for days.
'I forgive you,' he keeps saying,
'I forgive you.'"

"For what?"

"He never says."

The woman's voice broke and she sank to the bed
And ran her fingers over her husband's white arm.

"But there's something strange
         and terrible
Went on once. He never told me
But he'd wake up in the night sometimes
Cursing them and sobbing and saying,

'Get away, get away!' Just like that.
'Get away, get away!'
I've got my guess
But I wouldn't want to say.
That was a strange house your father
Grew up in, a strange house.
It left him with some kind of devil."

Again came the voice from the man on the bed.

"I forgive you."

Joanna's fingers found the bed frame and
        gripped it tight.
It was as if she had been peeping for years
Into a kaleidoscope and someone just jarred it.
She studied the new design.

"Daddy?" She spoke incredulously.
"Knowing how terrible it was,
Knowing how much pain it caused you,
You still *did it to me?*"

She stood before her father like a Greek heroine
Railing at the gods, fire in her eyes.

"Damn you, Daddy!
There is no excuse! You chose!
Yes and no were in front of you
And you put out your hand and chose!
I have two children and I have
Never done anything like that to them

And I never will!
I don't care how many fathers'
Fathers' fathers' fathers
Or uncles or mothers
Have done it! It was never okay!
And it ends with me, do you hear?"

She said it triumphantly, as if reading
A proclamation.

"It ends with me!"

Joanna fell sobbing to her knees
And grabbed her father's terrible, terrible hands
As if she would crush the life from them.
Her tears fell onto the thin fingers
And onto her own.

The man's head lifted a little and his eyes opened.

"Joanna? Joanna?"

Was the pain she saw hers or his
And would she ever know?

A little later, when Joanna went to the kitchen,
She paused for a moment in the hall
By the picture in the bamboo frame
The picture of Jesus standing in a white robe
By an open tomb.

HER FATHER'S TEARS

She was always embarrassed
When her father cried
For it was so unmanly
And she always knew
When it would happen.

When he read the note
From Mrs. Lewis
Saying what a joy she was
To have in class
And how proud of her
He must be

When they brought in
A fifty-candled cake
And sang him a surprise

When the six o'clock news
Showed the kidnapped returned
Or the hostage released
Or the flag at half mast

He would reach for his handkerchief
Folded and white
And dab his left eye
Then his right
And she would *just die*!

She grew up, of course, and would now
If she could reach across the years

Fill a flask
With the holy water
Of her father's tears.

NEW HANDS

Celia got drinking from her mother
And hitting from her father
And yelling from both
Like she got pizza crusts for breakfast.

And she took it all in
And digested it and became it
Because you are what you eat.

And her parents
Ate from the table of their parents
Who ate from the table of theirs
Back and back and back
And Celia was stuck.

But cells die
And every seven years we are new.

Celia's new heart and new hands
Set the table and stir the pot
And serve better stuff than she ever got.

WOMAN AGING

All her life she had been
A vegetable garden
Every inch rowed and planted
In corn, beans, carrots:
Producing
Nourishing
Doing.

Now some landscape architect
Has rearranged the space
Clearing, softening
Putting in a little pond
And a path and sand
Offering a quiet place
For being
For sitting on the one rock
And studying
The single lotus.

Pastel and thin
She is an Oriental meditation garden
Designed for going within.

STILL LIFE

The first thing she did
When she walked in the door
After the doctor talked about
Six months if she was lucky

Before she read the leaflet
Clutched in her hand on chemotherapy

Before she called her sister

Before she sat down on the couch and stared

She went to the back closet
And unwrapped the easel
And the oils that were still good
Which the children had given her
Several Christmases ago

And set them up in the kitchen
Where the afternoon light hit
Her little garden in a pot
Her little African violet.
She studied the seven purple flowers
With five golden knots
As though embroidered at each center.
She studied the thirteen green velvet leaves
And the underside where the vulnerable
Red veins ran.

She had never
Seen anything more beautiful

And she began.

A DREAM OF PEACE

I woke on the morning of last New Year's Eve
Holding a dream that had landed
Like a dove on my hand
And coaxing it to stay.

In my dream the Gorbachevs, Raisa and Mikhail,
Sat with me like fine old friends in my living room
And I in ecstacy said,
"Oh, Raisa, let us hold a conference of women
From all over the world and lead out toward peace!"

The thought was so beautiful that
Saying it, I burst into tears
Which stirred the dove on my hand
Which woke me up.

I am holding the conference.
Thousands of women from hundreds of countries
Come to raise the chalice of sisterhood,
To bury the sword.

We come under divine commission,
Visited with visions
Of a future and gentle Eden
Where woman and man can live again
Peaceful and equal in the garden.

We come armed with memories and myths:
The invention of brutality
The first metal that was struck to make the first war

The trading (foolish as for a mess of pottage)
Of cooperation for competition
Of partnership for domination.

We come armed with the knowledge that all weapons
Have been traded now for the last weapon.
There will be no better bow and arrow
No sharper sword, no bigger gun.
We have the last weapon
And we know that we have never yet invented
A weapon we haven't used.

And we sense somehow that the only way to
        avoid our end
Is to remember our beginning
To search the dark areas, unlike the drunk
Who looks for his lost key
Not on the steps where he dropped it
But on the porch because the light is better there.
We come resolved to find our lost key
In the darkness
In the patterns of antiquity before the fall.

We come armed with arms that embrace one another
With feet that cannot march for dancing
With mouths that cannot shout for singing.

We come, finally speaking the secret
That many have known but few have uttered:
We are not the weak ones.
We are not the second ones.
We are not removed from the important place,
Barred from the holy of holies.

We are at the center of the important place.
We are the fire in the holy of holies.
We are where it begins, where it is born and reborn.

And we know it is time now to raise our woman's arms
And pass the chalice indeed
And sip our sisterhood and pass it to our brothers
Who are weary, so weary of the sword
And humble enough now to look at their sisters
At their mothers and at their wives and say yes
Humble enough now to study the woman to learn
How life can be given and given again
To learn softness and sharing
And patience and pain and being.
Just being.

We come with doves in our dreams
And doves on our arms
And let them loose after a world-shaking song
And watch them fill the sky with wings of peace.

Women

And Their

Men

I SPEAK FOR ROMANTIC LOVE

I speak for romantic love
Like I speak for democracy.

The woman who sees her husband
For the first time when her veil moves
At the wedding
May learn to love him
But there is something totalitarian there
Something unadult.

As the human brain is beyond the amoeba
As the ballot is beyond the dictate
Romantic love is beyond arrangement.

It is revolutionary, as America is.
It is the full flower of liberty
Opening of its own
All voluntary, hands freely raised
Because I, *I* will and *I* must
And *I* stand-responsible for this great act
This wild, frontier adventure
Where *I* choose
Where there is not master and slave
And buyer and bought
Where both are created equal
And equally invest and equally commit
And pledge allegiance to each other
Loving by consent of the lovers.

Yes, it is individual and inconvenient.
Yes, it is messy and experimental

And dangerous and may occasionally
Counter the common good.

But I salute the flag of lovers.
There is no going back.
The blessed, the free
Set foot on this land
Choice above all other lands
Kiss the soil
And delirious, reckless
Dare the most magnificent
Pursuit of happiness.

WHAT YOU DO TO ME

"Recent medical literature
indicates people are healthier
when they're in love."

My darling
At the thought of you
The lactic acid in my blood drops
Making me less tired.

At your touch, my love
My endorphins increase
Producing a natural sense of
Well-being.

As your arms go around me
The lymphocytes go wild
In my blood
Strengthening my white cells.

And, oh
With your lips on mine
My limbic system is charged
And activity is increased
In all parts of my body.

And so, my love
I am grateful for you
From the bottom of my liver
And lungs and pancreas
And every other part

Not to mention, my love
My heart.

SABBATH

And you are
My sabbath, too.

I come to you for rest,
Renewal,
Come to worship God in you
And God in me.

Silently
As light through the religious reds
And blues and golds of glass
In a cathedral window
I come to you for peace.

ESSENCE OF LOVE

I splash your love on me
Like perfume
Lavish
The lovelier than lilac scent
Over wrists and temples
And neck.

Heads turn
As I walk.

FOCUS

Falling in love
Is a matter of focus
I believe
Like a movie camera that
Zooms in on a face
Leaving everyone else
Background and slightly
Blurred.

The story calls for it:
One face
Suddenly the only face.

Ingenious and
Absurd.

FILLING YOU

I want to fill my days
With filling you.

I am acres of wheat.
Let me harvest, mill
Mix, rise, bake, spread
With honey
And serve you
Breakfast in bed.

BEARABLE

I remember saying it,
"Oh, I am so happy!"
I remember that I could not
Not say it, I was so happy.

I remember
The flowers on the wallpaper
Your fingers on my face
How the gold flame
Of the white candle danced
And danced and how the words came
Because they could not
Not come,
"Oh, I am so happy!"

I see it, hear it, feel it
But through gauze.

Angels are assigned
A kindness, I do believe
To cover heaven and love
With a curtain
And blur them bearable
For those who look back.

LIKE MISTLETOE

Being in love
Like mistletoe
Is marvelous to kiss under
But, like mistletoe
It cannot feed itself.

No more photosyntheses
Is here in this
Unspeakably sweet passion
Than is in these clustered leaves
And shiny berries birds like.

A guest
Such as being in love
And mistletoe
Requires a host
Something with a good
Root system
Something solid
Like sycamore, oak
Or respect.

Pulled loose
From a rooted thing
Even tied with red ribbon
And hung for the laughing
Singing celebration
Mistletoe
And being in love
Are charmed and charming
But only good, finally
For a few kisses.

FOR A DAUGHTER IN LOVE

I would not walk on her happiness
Any more than I would
Walk on a brand new lawn.
It is too tender.

I will not tell her now.

She has fallen in love
And I will wait until she has gotten up
And is standing straight.

I will wait until she comes to me
With questions in her eyes like tears.

I will tell her then
Like we finally tell the person
Who is sent out of the room
In those silly games we used to play
Tell her what everybody else
Has known, each in their turn:

That falling in love is a trap
Whereby life snatches people by the two's
And ties them so tightly together
That they can't get away
Until they learn something
Learn about love, real love:
Being in, working in, living in
Rising in, all begun by
Falling in.

I hope she will be a good sport
And nod her head and even smile
And say,
"Okay."

MOTHER AND OTHER CHILD

After feeding him and the children
And picking up after him and the children
And instructing him and the children
  again how to scrape their plates

After scolding him and the children
  for fighting over the television
And pleading with him and the children
  to get their homework
  and their taxes done
And smiling at him and the children
  and saying cheerily, "Oh, Sweetheart,
  just try! I know you can do it!"

She attempted to find the word
For what she felt when he
Rolled over and reached for her breast.

He would not understand "incest."
She chose "tired."

FALLING OUT OF LOVE HAIKU

Blossoms fall to ground.
Find new tree still pink or wait
For September fruit.

". . . AND OBEY"

He was the god of her world
He told her:
She was under him
As he was under God
Which left her
She soon realized
Pretty far under.

The person who drinks downstream
Of the cattle herd
Is less likely to get a clear drink
Than the person upstream.

But he
Being the god of her world
Blessed her with groceries today
And eternal exaltation tomorrow
And without him, they both knew
Whatever would she do?

Now
If I had been on the jury
For the crimes he committed
To which she closed her eyes
She would have been guilty too
Of course.

And
I don't defend her
Dumbly watching for ten years as

Her husband's cool hands
Took off his belt
With the silver buckle
To beat the kids.

Nor
Do I excuse her
Returning her parents' letters
Unopened or telling her friends
They could not call
Or speaking things that were not true
Because her husband told her to
Or eating only fruit
And wearing sleeves that reached her wrists
And never cutting her hair
Because her little god decreed
What she could do, eat, wear.

But
I say it is time
And way past time
That every woman
Invite herself upstream
Where the air is sharp
And the water is clean.

SHOPPER

He works until he drops.

She shops.

And for the hot tub
Teak bedroom set from Hong Kong
Oriental rugs
And Gucci pumps
She has not yet bought

His life insurance
Helps a lot.

AFTER THE MASTECTOMY

They were afraid it would be different
To make love without
Her breast on
And it was.

Right from the start
It brought him closer
To her heart.

FLAWS

She was fed up
And ready to pack her bags
And might have hauled out the Samsonite
That very morning if she hadn't read
In the Sunday supplement how
Michaelangelo made the David
Out of a block of marble so flawed
That other sculptors passed it by.

So instead of leaving him a note
Telling him to go to hell
She sat in their room
In the reclining chair
Thinking up one nice thing to say
Which was that he always had clean hair
And then remembered too
That he was sweet to the kids
And that he laughed at her jokes
And that he didn't like his job
But every morning got up anyway.

And she remembered too
That she usually burned carrots
And didn't smell so great
In the mornings
And could stand to lose thirty pounds
And even her kids said
She'd forgotten how to play.

For two hours and a half
She sat there
Studying her marble
And measuring and figuring
And dreaming and sharpening her tools
For one more day.

SPLIT

You felt safe
I know
In that little space
Laced with love.
Your coccoon
You called it
Warm
Warm.
I cried with you
When it split.

Oh, safe
Cannot compare with sky.
I like you so much better
As a butterfly.

RADICAL

She could discuss issues
With the best of them
And did her part for the causes
Absolutely

But sometimes she left early
During refreshments
Or before the envelopes
Were all stamped
To go to another meeting

And her friends never guessed
She hurried home
Where
In a matter of hours

With one wonderful man
She established peace
Justice and equality
Ended hunger
And observed the triumph
Of love.

CARLA AND JIM

Carla and Jim
Fell in love over a cadavar
In pre-med biology
And he joked that he
Found the liver and lost his heart
That day in the lab.

They went to movies and studied after
And ate pizza and studied during
And made out and studied before
And then grades came
And she got an A and he got a B
And he didn't look into
Her brown eyes quite the same
Anymore.

Carla is thirty-five and still single
And she glances at her
Biological clock now and then
And tries to turn off the alarm
And she stitches up
And listens to the lungs and hearts
Of other people's children.

Jim works hard in X-Ray
And goes home hassled and harried
To his four children—
The three little boys they had
And the lovely girl he married.

POSITION

If "A" looks up to "B"
Then by nature of the physical universe
"B" must look down on "A"
Rather like two birds
Positioned
One on a tree
And one on the ground.

Or so thought Marjorie
Who had always wanted to marry
A man she could look up to
But wondered where that
Would place *her*
If she did.

Imagine her astonishment
When she met Michael and found
That together they stood
Physics on its head.

You could never
Draw this on paper
For it defies design

But year after year
They lived a strange
Arrangement
That by all known laws
Could not occur:

She looked up to him
And he looked up to her.

SUPPORTIVE WIFE

Her job was to be
A supportive wife

And so

Sometimes holding a noose
Around his neck

Sometimes working the strings
That played his ankles and elbows

Sometimes steadying the crutches
She placed under his arms

She stood
Supporting him as best she could.

WRONG, RIGHT?

You are clearly wrong
And I am clearly right.

But I will support
Your being wrong
Which is clearly the right
Thing for me to do

Because after all
Being wrong may be
Right for you
And it would be
Wrong of me
To make you right.

So be wrong as long
As you want to.
It's quite all right.

SUTTEE FOR RICHARD'S WIFE

For twenty-seven years
She had called herself
"Richard's wife."
He was the first, last
Only thing in her
Very full life.

Two weeks after the day
She first called herself
"Richard's widow"
She went up in fire:

The car and the cliff
Her funeral pyre.

TURNING

I turn
But not away.

Toward
(Like a sunflower)
Light
Warmth.
I turn toward life.

The decision
Is in my roots
And is deep.

You are free
To face the ground
If you have no will
To lift
And I will be sad.

I am willing to be sad
But not to be dead
And so I turn.

TO THE TRUTH:
INVITATION THAT WAS NEVER SENT

Harold and Ilene Bradley
invite you to a garden reception
at their home to help them celebrate
fifty years of enduring to the end
even though
the end should have come
after the first year when it became clear
that they did not love each other
or particularly like each other
and had very little in common
and actually brought out the worst in each other
but were
too frightened to cut their losses
and move on.

She
in fact
remarked on their twenty-fifth anniversary
as they were eating seafood
"Do you think the next twenty-five years
will be as bad as the last twenty-five?"
and indeed they were.

Your presence will be present enough
just as their presence has been
all that
Harold and Ilene
have given each other these many years.

One until five p.m.
August nineteenth

THE RAIN AND THE GROUND

He was the rain
And I love him for this.
He brought the flowers
I knew they were his.

He moved over me
A gentle storm
The rain was sweet
And the rain was warm

And the flowers came
And the flowers grew.
That he brought the flowers
Was all that I knew.

Drought has come
And drought has burned
But nature teaches
And I have learned:

I am the ground
No matter the skies.
Oh, I bring the flowers
And the flowers will rise.

LETTING GO

I did it just like
The counselor said.
I closed my eyes
And saw myself on the pier
You on the boat
A rope between
Tied waist to waist.

> "And now untie your end
> Of the rope, slowly."

It felt like hemp in my hand
But I knew it was not.
Every fiber was an event
A laugh, a kiss, a fight
A prayer, a birth, a joke
A tear, all braided together
And tight.

> "Let it go.
> It's time to let go."

I looked at the boat
And could not read your face
In the shadow of the sail.

Through my hands
And into the water—
All that laughter
Those prayers
Tears, kisses in the water.

I would have jumped in
To save them
Like children overboard
But they were water
In the water now
And the boat was moving
And you were waving goodbye.

"Let go. It's through."

The boat bobbed
Further and further

And I waved too.

NOT A PAIR

Alison agreed
To become part of a couple
Not half of a pair.

A pair of skiis
Must ride the slope
Without a deviation
And if one makes
An independent motion
The jig is up.

A pair of socks
Must cling together
In the wash
And if one takes a spin
With the sheets or the towels
The other sits on the shelf
Flat and waiting for its match
To show up with the next batch.

Alison had been paired
Before and it scared
The daylights out of her to even think
Of linking up with anyone.

She had been a sock lost in the wash
Had been a ski that caused upsets on the slope,
And she wasn't now about
To become a glove.

But she loved him
And he loved her
And they decided "couple"
Was a word roomy enough
That they could both live in it.
It had two syllables, anyway
Instead of one
And it even sounded like dancing
Which, these days
Lets you be
Both together and free

All
Over the hall.

UNBORN

That he and she
Could have been we
Is nothing unusual
In a world full of fields
That could have been flowers.

Unborn beauty runs
As far as the eye can see.
And there is he
And here is she.

Occasionally
They almost sense
The almost scent
Of the almost blossom
And have to
Catch their breath.

SHE WAITED

These are the games
That kept her alive:

Every time she saw a taxi
Within a mile of her house before dark
If it was not raining
It would be him
Come to surprise her
And to stay.

Every time the phone rang
On a Sunday night after nine o'clock
If she'd gone to church
It would be him.
"Darling, it's all worked out.
I'll be there soon,"
He would say.

Every time she heard the mailbox squeak
If there were three letters or more
And all of them were white
One would be from him
Telling her he had his ticket
And would be there the next day.

Every time she heard a car door
By the side entrance of the rest home
If they'd served chicken for supper
And she'd taken her pills
It would be him
Smelling of Old Spice and smiling
And come to dance her away.

SECOND WEDDING

This time a woman
Not a girl

A necklace
Not a pearl

An orchard in September
Not a branch in May

Abundant with a hundred
Tumbling loves
Fruited and golden
To gift a man

She says "I do"
And knows "I can."

LAST TOUCH

When she touched him for the first time
His skin was warm
And his hair was soft
And his fingers sweet
And the sun through the tall pines
Rose in invocation
On the blanket of blossoms
And he was so beautiful
And she had never seen such a smile.

When she touched him for the last time
His skin was cold
And his hair was thin
And his fingers shook
And the moon through the hospital window
Fell in benediction
On the little table
Heavy with flowers and fruit
And her tear joined his tear
At the little line
Where his smile began.

Women

AND THEIR

CHILDREN

BANKERS

He works at the bank
And has a large desk
And people listen when he talks.

And he takes good care
Of his charges:
Money, certificates
Stocks.

And she stays home
Unnoticed
And every day
Tends treasures
That outshine all the gold
In Fort Knox.

MATRIARCHAL BLESSING

I have blessed you
You know

Not hands on head
But body around body
Nine months encircled
By the liquid sound
Of my light

Uttering not promises
But miracles cell by cell

Giving not admonitions
But affirmations of your
Natural splendor

You wear
You are my blessing
A blessing I author
By the power of the holy
That I bear
And that I share
By love ordained
And through which I
Pronounce you
Blessed forever.

MOTHERLOAD

Motherhood has ruined me for life.

I want to nurse the world
A continent to a breast.

I want to cut up waffles
For all the third world
Send the dictator to his room
Ground the drug dealers
Wash out the pornographers'
Mouths with soap
And spray organized crime
With Black Flag.

I want to make all the politicians
And all the executives sit on the couch
And memorize the golden rule
And stand up and say it in unison.

I want to grab a bullhorn
And announce to the world
That the barbecues will stop
Until all the litter—*all* the litter—
Has been picked up.

Oh, I could fix everything
If they would all just listen to me,
Listen to me,
Listen to me!

I have such illusions of grandeur:
I am a mother.

CHILD MAKING

She knew that if she had to
Hand-make this child

She would probably end up
With something like
The dress with the huge arm holes
She hid half finished
In the bottom drawer

Or the plaque on the kitchen wall
From which beans and corn
Kept dropping:

A child
With far too much skin
Or eyebrows
That just would not stay on.

So she lay back
And day after day
Knitted away
On little booties
      (uneven but sweet)

Glad she had help
In making the feet.

AARON'S OTHER WOMAN

Clearly it takes
Two generations of women
To civilize a man.

I took him past
Throwing food on the floor
Peeing in public places
Saying bad words
Spitting on the sidewalk
And playing on the escalators.

But I could never
In a million mother years
Take him the quantum leap
This seventeen year-old girl
With the wispy telephone voice
And the lavendar eyelids
Has taken him in one week:

Taken him by a slim
And bracleted arm
Past belching, grunting
Scowling, snapping

And into smiling, sweetness
Singing
And infinite charm.

IN CELEBRATION
OF THE
FIRST MENSTRUATION

Katy,
Who has of late been putting
Pads and panties
On her Keeshond dog
Briget Baby Brown Eyes,
Loped long-legged and twelve and sweet
Into my room today and giggled,
"Mom, Mom, I'm in heat!
I just started!"

I pulled her down
Into the big chair that we
Used to not quite fill
And made sure she understood
That a menstruating woman
Is of the devil
That she must not
Look at the sun, sit in water
Speak to a man
For she is unclean
Or enter a church
For she would defile it.

And I stroked her
Innocent freckled skin
And bright braided hair
And told her to keep in mind
That she is, as St. Jerome said,
Formed of foul slime.

Katy laughed. "Right, Mom!"

And I told her all that was from
A bad period
Men's period
When male was god and jealous
And said what was what
A period that luckily menopaused.

But that there was an earlier time
When woman's secret was sacred
When the Great Goddess
Gave the blood of life
And all worshipped joyously
At her royal fountain
When girls "bore the flower"
A flower that flows a future fruit
Making her a marvel
A time that is due again.

Then I gave Katy five and said,
"Hey, woman, let's go celebrate!"
And we went right out under the sun
And Katy spoke right up to the man
And ordered a BLT and we ate.

We clicked our cups to flowering
And Katy giggled and blushed and bounced
And blessed the restaurant
With her presence.

CHRIST CHILDREN

Let us make you a child again
For Christmas.
Let us put you in the cradle
As we put Jesus in the manger
Pre-crucifixion and sweet
With just born eyes that meet
The wonder of star and smile.

For a little while
Let us make you children again.
Here there are no nails
In your innocence.
Here there is over you
A sky bursting bright
And under you the breast of a mother
Softer than hay.

You will not stay
I know
And Jesus will have to go
To Golgotha:
His little hands were born
To bear a cross.
And you, my darling,
Came to the same sad world
Where trust is lost
At the hands of those who
Know not what they do.

At the end of the story
The Christ will rise
And so will you.

But let us make you
Children again for Christmas
(The Christ children that you are)
Touched only by swaddling
And the light of a star.

CHILD-RAISING SEMINAR

Under the tent at the state fair
Two hundred people
Stood smiling and cheering
As the new-born calf
On little stick feet
Jacked himself inches up
And tumbled to the sawdust
And then
        blinking
                wobbling
Tried again
        and again
                and again.

And when he was finally up
All feet on the floor
The cheers became a roar

And I went home
And practiced
Smiling and clapping
For my own stumbling four.

DON'S DAUGHTER

I celebrate the birth
Of this girl child
With the joy
Of a Hebrew celebrating
The birth of a boy.

With tambourines
Or cards or calls
Her birth
Is worth
Celebrating:

See how her mother smiles
          (Though that is no surprise)
But, oh
See how her father
Kneels at the cradle
Of this little goddess
With worship in his eyes!

FOREVER CHILD

She holds her big girl
Across her lap on the couch:
Rocking chairs were not made
For children who will be
Forever children.

She spins words of comfort
Like a song—
Maybe tomorrow, maybe tomorrow,
Maybe tomorrow it will be possible

To stand up in the roller skates

To speak words that others understand

To find a friend who would like to
Go to a movie this weekend

Maybe tomorrow, maybe tomorrow.
Lullabies were not written
For children who will be
Forever children.

And she looks out the window
At the darkening sky
And closes her eyes and prays again
That she will outlive her sweet baby:

The world was not made
For children who will be
Forever children.

CLEAN

The baby she wore to the wedding
Under the lace
Became her sin offering.

And the energy she bent
Toward keeping him clean was more
Than she spent
On the vaccuuming
And the dishes and the laundry.

He knew not to touch himself
Before he knew how to walk
And he never took off his shirt
Even in August in the sandbox
And when the guys showed him
Pictures of girls
He did the right thing and left
And vomited in the gutter
On the way home.

At fifty-four he lives alone
And always has
Except for the cats
Whose numbers vary

And his mother kneels and prays
That the right woman will come along
For her son to marry.

ON PURPOSE

The little girl unfrowned and then
Sort of smiled when
After hearing the dictionary definition

She was told that what adopted
Really meant was

Searched for
Prayed for
Worked for
Finally gratefully got
Unquestionably on purpose
And loved a lot.

MOTHER'S POST PLEDGE

Look,
I hereby:

Cross out my critique
        of your performance,
Toss out my agenda
        for your life,
Tear up my list of
        things you need to do,
Swear up and down
        I will not do it again.

Of course it's odd,
But for a while there
I mistook myself for God.

DON'T PUSH

The minute the doctor said "push,"
I did, and I've got to stop now
Because you're eighteen.

Breathe deeply
Think of something else
Don't push
Don't push.

FOR CHILDREN GROWN AND GONE

My garden could not contain
The beauty of you.

I watched you blossom
Then burst into blessings,
Seeds winging in the wind
Beyond my field.

Only God can measure the yield
Or knows
All the places where
Your beauty grows.

JOHN LEAVES HOME

Surely you're not going without me?
Surely you're not taking your stereo
And leaving your mother?
Surely, John, a policeman will find you
And bring you home.
We're not finished!

I read to you "The Little Red Hen"
And talked about industry.
I read to you "Animal Farm"
And talked about equality.
But I have not read to you yet
"Les Miserables"
Or the complete works of Shakespeare,
And if I don't
Who will?

I have discussed with you at the dinner table
My hundreds of news clippings
On American-Russian relations
Acts of heroism or horror
The birth of a panda
And Ann Landers' columns on
Drug abuse, sending thank you notes
And teenage pregnancy.
But next month and the next
Newspapers will come out
And if I don't scour them for things
You need to know about
Who will?

I have made you turn off the TV
Left a list of important things to be done
In your blue color-coded notebook
On the kitchen counter:
"Mow lawn, sweep back deck, vacuum bedroom,
Write letter to grandparents, get haircut."
But the days will continue to come
With their twenty-four hours
And if I do not write out for you
A list of important things to do
Who will?

Ah, you are laughing.

Oh, John, take me with you.
Tuck a little mother in your head
And every now and then let her speak.

Take me with you.
You need to cease being a child
But I need always to be a mother
And if you won't let me
Who will?

RAJA MOTHERHOOD

It starts with
Meditation on the toes of a baby
And leads to spiritual exercise
That would break the best yogi
Sitting cross-legged before his lotus:

Serenity
And colic
And three hours sleep last night

Grace
And the puppy feces
On the new carpet

Charity
And screams
In the grocery store when the
Oreos are ripped from white knuckles

Harmony
And three Halloween costumes
By tomorrow morning:
A clown, a witch
And a washing machine
To go with Stacey's dryer.

Honor
And another conference
With the teacher
And possibly the principal

Silence
And the roar of motorbike
And rock
And tap shoes on kitchen tile

Acceptance
And all that is dear
Packing up and leaving home

Path to god-consciousness
All begun by
Meditation on the toes of a baby.